Revise a

Commerce 1

D J Thomas MA BSc(Econ) PhD

Series Adviser: Geoffrey Whitehead

Pitman

PITMAN PUBLISHING LIMITED
128 Long Acre, London WC2E 9AN

PITMAN PUBLISHING INC
1020 Plain Street, Marshfield, Massachusetts 02050

Associated Companies
Pitman Publishing Pty Ltd, Melbourne
Pitman Publishing New Zealand Ltd, Wellington
Copp Clark Pitman, Toronto

© D J Thomas 1985

First published in Great Britain 1985

British Library Cataloguing in Publication Data
Thomas, D. J. (Derek John)
  Revise and test commerce 1.—(Revise and test)
  1. Commerce—Examinations, questions, etc.
  I. Title   II. Series
  380.1'076   HF1008

  ISBN 0–273–02142–7

Printed at The Bath Press, Avon

Contents

Using this Revise and Test booklet

1   The 'Revise and Test' series is in question and answer form. It will teach you everything you need to know (we hope) about your particular syllabus. The questions are detailed and rigorous, and cannot be answered always with one word answers. It follows that the first time you go over a topic you will be learning the material rather than testing yourself. It is not just a self-testing book, but a self-teaching book too!

2   The first time you study a topic you may need to go over it 2 or 3 times. Then put a tick against the topic number in the check list at the back of the book.

3   Subsequently you should revise the topic at intervals, especially just before a monthly test or an examination. Each time you revise it put a further tick.

4   If you find a topic particularly difficult put a ring round the number. This will remind you to do it again soon. Practice makes perfect.

5   Finally remember that learning facts is relatively easy. Applying them in written work is more difficult. Each topic has one piece of written work and you should find others from textbooks and past examination papers. Remember the saying 'Writing maketh an exact man'. Don't worry about who is going to mark your written work. You can appraise it for yourself! Keep writing!

1 Producers and consumers

1 Why do people go to work?

People work to earn money for the purpose of satisfying wants.

2 Name three basic wants

Food and drink, clothing and shelter.

3 Once people have their essential needs, do they stop wanting things?

No — things are scarce in relation to the desire for them. Most people would like better houses, more domestic appliances, more holidays abroad and so on. There seems to be an inexhaustible desire for more and better goods and services.

4 What is a consumer?

Someone who buys goods and services to satisfy wants.

5 What determines a person's standard of living?

The amount of goods and services that he or she may consume.

6 What is a producer?

Someone who engages in the production of goods or the provision of services. For example, a miner produces coal; a solicitor provides legal services.

7 What is the purpose of production?

To satisfy consumers' wants through the provision of goods and services.

8 When is the production process complete?

The aim of production is to satisfy consumer's wants and this is not achieved until the product is in the possession of the consumer, or the service has been enjoyed by the consumer. The work of distributing goods from factories and docks is undertaken by wholesalers and retailers. The work of bringing consumers to enjoy services is performed by transport, and other services are also involved.

9 What are the four branches of production?

Primary production, secondary production and the two branches of tertiary production: commercial services and personal services.

10 What is primary production?

Work concerned with the extraction of materials made available by nature, or with agriculture, forestry, fishing and animal husbandry.

11 What is secondary production?

Work concerned with the manufacture of raw materials into finished products; and assembling finished products into new forms.

12 Name four examples of extractive industries

Coal-mining, oil drilling, gold crushing, natural gas extraction.

13 Name five examples of manufacturing industries

Textiles, metal manufacture, chemicals, food processing, cigarette manufacture.

14 What is the work of the construction industry?

To build finished products such as houses, schools, factories and industrial plant from raw materials such as bricks, tiles, door frames, window frames, glass and other semi-manufactured products.

15 Give three additional examples of construction industries

Road-making, dock and harbour construction and railway construction.

16 What is trade?

Trade means the exchange of raw materials and finished products by buying and selling in either home or foreign markets through retail, wholesale, import and export organisations.

17 What is commerce?

Trade and all services which assist trade.

18 What are the divisions of commerce?

Retail and wholesale trades; import and export trades; warehousing; transport; communications; insurance; banking; advertising; and market research.

19 What is the purpose of commercial activity?

(a) To assist the movement of raw materials to industry and the distribution of finished goods from industry to consumers. (b) To move people to places where they can take advantage of personal services.

20 How does warehousing assist trade?

Warehouses provide storage facilities for goods until they are required. Many goods have a seasonal demand; for example, summer clothes made during the winter months must be stored until consumers wish to buy. Warehousing also assists marketing by bringing many products together under one roof, for display, sale and distribution.

21 How does banking assist trade?

(a) Indirectly, by collecting the capital which enables production to take place and make goods available. (b) Directly by providing the cheque system and other means of payment for goods; financial assistance in the form of bank loans to traders who buy and hold stocks and by providing a safe place for cash takings.

22 How does advertising and market research assist trade?

Advertising provides consumers with information about goods available for sale and seeks to promote sales by persuading people to try them or to buy more. Market researchers measure the potential demand for goods and thereby assist manufacturers to match the supply of products with the demand for them.

23 What is the chain of production?

The sequence of activities that starts with people's 'wants' and ends with the satisfaction of those wants. The links in the chain are wants, enterprise, production, transport and distribution, exchange, consumption, satisfaction – and in a short while, 'wants' again.

Written Exercise: *Explain how commercial activities change the ownership and location of goods.*

Go over the topic again until you are sure of all the answers. Then tick it off on the check list at the back of the book.

2 The factors of production

1 What are the factors of production?

They are the resources available for producing goods and services. They comprise labour, land and capital. Production usually requires a combination of these factors. In order to achieve this, there is a fourth factor called 'enterprise'. Without its managing and coordinating function, the other factors would be idle and unused.

2 What is a person called who shows enterprise?

An entrepreneur.

3 What is the factor called labour?

It is the human resource. The supply of labour available for production is the total number of people of working age. The size of the labour force is determined by (a) the size of the total population, (b) the age distribution of the population, and (c) the social arrangements in the country concerned particularly the time spent in education and whether women are allowed to work other than domestically.

4 What is the factor called land?

Land comprises all kinds of natural resources such as soil, mineral deposits, fisheries, forests and climatic conditions (such as sunshine, wind and rain). It provides the site on which production can take place; and the supply of raw materials used in the production of goods.

In their original state, natural resources are a gift of nature. Thus land, in the economic sense, is unimproved land. In a modern industrial society, unimproved land is relatively rare and most areas of land embody some capital which has been used in the past to improve it.

5 What is capital when considered as a factor of production?

It is not money, the common meaning of capital. It is a stock of assets which have been created in the past to help with production, such as factory buildings, industrial plant, power stations, tools and equipment and transport facilities. These resources are often called 'producer goods' or 'capital assets'.

6 What does the entrepreneur do?

He/she organises the use of land, labour and capital for production and bears the risks involved. The entrepreneur is the one who runs an enterprise.

7 What sort of risks are involved in production?

Not so much the ordinary risks such as fire, burglary, road accidents, etc., which can be covered by insurance. The risks are non-insurable – for example, the risk of making things that no one wants, or which can only be sold at a loss.

8 How are the factors of production rewarded?

In return for its part in producing goods and services, each factor receives an income. Labour is paid a wage or salary; land earns rent; capital is rewarded by interest; and the reward of the entrepreneur is profit.

9 Explain the process by which production is started

Entrepreneurs use capital to hire land and labour to create the basic capital assets (factories, production lines, tools, etc.). When these are ready, entrepreneurs hire labour and buy raw materials to make finished goods. Income from sales of these goods is used to buy more factors of production, to pay interest on the original capital and provide profit for the entrepreneur.

Written Exercise: *Describe the factors of production that a small engineering firm would require to start up production of components for sale to a motor vehicle manufacturer.*

Go over the topic again until you are sure of all the answers. Then tick it off on the check list at the back of the book.

3 Specialisation and the division of labour

1 What is manufacture of standardised articles on a large scale called?

Mass production of goods.

2 What does mass production depend upon?

The division of labour and specialisation.

3 What is division of labour?

A system of dividing up the production of an article into a large number of different operations which can be done by different workers. The system is seen most clearly in industries which make durable consumer goods such as cars, electrical appliances, radio and television sets. These industries use assembly lines and as the products move slowly down the lines, each worker performs a particular task. The finished product at the end of the line is the result of the combined efforts of many specialist workers.

4 How did the process of division of labour develop?

(a) It began by dividing the day's work among the members of a family. (b) As towns grew it developed into specialisation by trades (butchers, bakers, wheelwrights, etc.). (c) The factory system enabled manufacturing to be broken down into various processes. (d) National trading led to specialisation in regions and localities. (e) International trade led to international specialisation – Swiss watches, Japanese cameras, French wines, etc. Each country specialises in the things it does best.

5 Is specialisation restricted to workers?

No – there is specialisation by *industry* such as the textile industry, the coal industry and so on. Within each industry *firms* specialise. Thus in the motor industry, there are firms which specialise in m' ' ing tyres, or batteries, or wheels or other components used in the production of a vehicle.

6 How many specialised jobs are there?

The Standard Industrial Classification drawn up by the Department of Employment lists over 30 000 different occupations.

7 Why is division of labour applied in industry?

(a) Higher output is possible. (b) Better use can be made of employees' differing experiences and abilities. For example, the creation of a large number of different jobs involving varying degrees of difficulty means that people are able to do tasks for which they are best suited. (c) No time is lost between the performance of the various processes, as would happen if one person was responsible for making the complete product. (d) Output can be measured accurately. If the assembly line is moving at a given speed, so many products will be coming off the line every hour. Thus a day's or a month's or a year's output can be estimated fairly accurately.

8 What are the benefits of specialisation among employees?

(a) Repetition of the same operation increases skill and more work can be done during the working day. (b) Jobs can be described more precisely (e.g. lathe operator, filing clerk) and the advertising of jobs and recruitment of staff is made easier. (c) A job takes a shorter time to learn and people are less reluctant to train for a new job.

9 Are there any disadvantages to the division of labour?

Yes. (a) A worker who performs the same task for a number of hours each day is, sooner or later, going to find the work monotonous. (b) Goods produced are usually standardised products, as can be seen in the design of cars, domestic appliances and houses. Whether or not standardisation is a disadvantage is really a matter of opinion. After all, consumers can pay extra for houses or cars built to their particular requirements. (c) Instability of employment may be a consequence. Workers in one industry are often dependent on those before them in the process of production. Thus a prolonged stoppage in the coal or steel industries may throw thousands of other workers out of work because supplies of raw materials stop. The same is true within an industry. Interdependence in car manufacture is such that the decision of a handful of workers to strike can put thousands of employees out of work within a short time.

10 Are there limitations to the division of labour?

Yes. The extent to which specialisation can be applied is dependent upon (a) a suitable system of exchange and (b) the extent of the market.

11 What is the meaning of 'exchange'?

If A spends all his time making cars and B spends all her time growing carrots, A has too many cars and no carrots, and B has plenty of carrots but no cars. The fruits of production have to be exchanged. People will specialise only if they can easily exchange the goods they make or the service they provide for goods and services made by other people.

12 How are exchanges arranged?

In a modern economy, those who have supplied a factor to make production possible are paid in money. They exchange this income for a wide range of goods and services produced by others.

13 How is specialisation affected by the extent of the market?

Only a large market will justify mass production with a high degree of specialisation. Thus the ready-to-wear fashion trades can grade clothes into a few standard sizes, and use uniform materials and standard accessories to mass produce garments. By contrast, *haute couture* and bespoke tailoring serve a personalised market where the division of labour cannot be applied to the same extent. The extent of the market depends also upon good transport facilities for the distribution of goods. Developments in sea and air transport have made possible the division of labour on an international scale. Countries specialise in producing a few only of the things that they could produce, and exchange their surplus requirements for the surpluses of goods produced by other countries.

Written Exercise: *Each day a brain surgeon is driven to the hospital by a chauffeur in a mass-produced car. What different aspects of the division of labour does each part of the statement imply?*

Go over the topic again until you are sure of all the answers. Then tick it off on the check list at the back of the book.

4 Types of shops

1 What does 'retail' mean?

The word means to cut up, or cut off again. Retailing requires the breaking down of large quantities into smaller quantities or bulk supplies into single items. It is the principal service given by a retailer. Cases of goods ('wholes') are bought from wholesalers and split up into smaller quantities that will suit customers.

2 What are the four main functions of a retailer?

To provide goods (a) that customers want; (b) at the time customers want them; (c) in the quantities customers require, and (d) locally, i.e. close to customers' homes.

3 In addition to these four main functions, retailers provide several services. List these services

(a) Delivery of goods. (b) Ordering of goods not in stock. (c) Advice on purchases. (d) Credit. (e) Repair or alteration of goods.

4 How do small shops survive the competition from bigger shops?

(a) A friendly, informal atmosphere appeals to many people. (b) Informal credit may be available. (c) Shops have a convenient local situation. (d) Opening times are flexible. (e) Membership of voluntary chains and the use of cash and carry warehouses allow price reductions to meet competition from bigger shops.

5 Why are department stores attractive to shoppers?

(a) A 'collection of shops' under one roof offers a wide choice of goods. (b) Services such as travel agencies, restaurants and hairdressing salons are available. (c) Credit accounts may be opened. (d) There is a delivery service and orders may be placed by post or telephone. (e) Shoppers can wander at leisure in comfortable and luxurious surroundings.

6 How is a department store organised?

There are merchandise departments and service departments. Merchandise departments sell the vast range of goods available in the store, and the people in charge are called buyers. The service departments are controlled by managers, and support the work of the merchandise departments. Three examples of service departments are clerical and accounting; stock reception, warehousing and transport; and maintenance.

7 What is the difference between a variety chain store and a specialist chain store?

A variety chain store, e.g. Woolworths, is a large store selling a wide variety of goods. A specialist chain store, e.g. Dolcis concentrates on the sale of a narrower range of goods such as shoes or food.

8 Why is a chain of shops in a better competitive position than a small shop?

(a) Having nation-wide branches of the same organisation ensures that goodwill is maximised – wherever people are they look for the well-tried commodity in the well-known place. (b) Buying is on a large scale and huge orders can command large discounts. (c) Specialist staff can be employed and proper training can be given. (d) Slow selling stocks in one area may be transferred to another where demand is high. (e) All branches are unlikely to suffer from a period of bad trade at the same time. Thus losses at a few branches can be carried while there is an overall profit. By contrast, a small shop goes out of business if trading losses occur.

9 State three ways in which big shops can purchase stock at reduced prices

(a) Bulk buying from independent manufacturers on a world-wide scale. (b) By setting up their own factories to manufacture at competitive rates. (c) By working with manufacturers to produce goods made to the retailer's own specification.

10 Why is self-service adopted by shops?

(a) It raises turnover because customers serve themselves. (b) It reduces staff levels and saves wages. (c) It enables expensive mechanised and computerised tills to be used economically. (d) A full range of goods on display encourages impulse buying.

11 Why are supermarkets popular with shoppers?

(a) All goods are plainly on view and prices are clearly marked. (b) Prices are relatively low due to a high volume of sales and bulk buying. (c) A wide range of goods is available. (d) There is no pressure from sales-conscious assistants. (e) There are no delays in waiting to be served.

12 How do hypermarkets differ from supermarkets?

They differ in size, position and price levels. Hypermarkets have a larger total floor area and a wider variety of goods. They are located away from town centres to cater for car-borne shoppers. Bulk purchases enable hypermarkets to cut prices below those of other shops.

Written Exercise: *What do you understand by 'large-scale retailing'? Explain why this type of retailing has grown in recent years.*

Go over the topic again until you are sure of all the answers. Then tick it off on the check list at the back of the book.

5 Retailing without shops

1 State five forms of retailing without shops

Local retail markets; doorstep selling; mail order; mobile shops; vending machines.

2 Why are prices in local retail markets likely to be lower than shop prices?

Stall-holders do not have the same expenses as shopkeepers (e.g. the latter pay heating and lighting bills) and their other overhead expenses are low. Their attitudes are competitive, and they buy stocks at 'bargain' prices.

3 What is 'doorstep selling'?

Direct selling to customers in their homes rather than through shops. Direct sales firms sell on a door-to-door basis or through 'selling parties'. Types of products sold include cosmetics, lingerie and plastic householder containers.

4 What is 'party selling'?

Coffee parties are held in private houses to which friends and neighbours of the hostess are invited. An agent of the selling firm attends to display examples of the firm's products. Orders are taken and the hostess receives a gift for providing hospitality.

5 What is the appeal of 'party selling' to consumers?

(a) Product demonstration in the home. (b) The opportunity to choose products at leisure. (c) Availability of guidance on the suitability and usefulness of the products. (d) A pleasant social occasion where a convivial atmosphere prevails.

6 Are there any drawbacks to consumers of this form of retailing?

Yes. Among neighbours and friends, consumers may find difficulty in refusing to buy and may end up with unwanted purchases, or unsuitable items.

7 Who sells by mail order?

Manufacturers; wholesalers; department stores; and general mail-order firms which operate through part-time agents.

8 How does the Post Office assist mail-order firms?

The Post Office provides a parcels delivery service and payment facilities on delivery (COD) for customers. Payment may also be made by postal order and by National Girobank facilities.

9 Why is mail order popular with consumers?

(a) Goods are available to people living far from shops or unable to visit shops. (b) Purchases are made at leisure and in the privacy of the home. (c) Easy and informal credit is available. (d) Merchandise can be viewed and handled before purchase. (e) The difficulties of town shopping (e.g. traffic congestion, parking problems) are avoided. (f) There are opportunities to become an agent and earn commission.

10 Are there any drawbacks to customers of mail order?

Yes. (a) There is no personal contact between retailer and customer. (b) Customers may find difficulty in judging the quality of goods from catalogues. (c) Prices may be higher than those charged by some shops.

11 How are mobile shops useful to consumers?

(a) They are convenient in that the shop comes to the consumer. (b) They may operate outside normal shop opening hours. (c) They serve areas often out of range of normal shopping facilities.

12 How is their usefulness limited?

(a) Choice, inevitably, is narrow because of the need to carry only popular, fast-selling lines of merchandise in order to make the most of the restricted space. (b) Prices may be high in a non-competitive situation.

13 What incentives are there for retailers to install automatic vending machines?

(a) They provide a useful addition to sales outside normal shopping hours. (b) Sales at fixed prices ensure a steady profit margin. (c) They can carry lines not normally sold in a particular retail situation (e.g. fish and chip shops may vend chocolate, sweets and canned drinks).

Written Exercise: *Explain why non-shop retailing is so popular with consumers.*

Go over the topic again until you are sure of all the answers. Then tick it off on the check list at the back of the book.

6 Money

1 What is money?

Something which is generally acceptable as a means of exchange.

2 How did exchange take place before the invention of money?

By barter, that is, the direct exchange of goods or services for other goods or services.

3 What are the drawbacks of barter?

(a) Exchange is dependent upon a 'double coincidence of wants', i.e. a person who wants to barter has to find someone who has something acceptable to exchange and who is also willing to accept the item offered. (b) The items bartered must be of equal value before a transaction can take place. (c) The exchange of large indivisible items is difficult to arrange. Many 'goods' cannot be easily subdivided – for example, a horse.

4 Why can primitive societies manage without a full money system?

Because they are largely self-sufficient. People do not buy their everyday needs and barter is satisfactory for the few items they do buy for special occasions.

5 Summarise the early stages in the development of money

(a) Commodities such as grain, cattle and salt were the first types of money. (b) Then came precious metals (gold and silver). (c) Then we had predetermined weights of precious metal in the form of coins.

6 Name the main types of money used in a modern economy

(a) Coins of non-precious metals, with no intrinsic value. (b) Banknotes. (c) Bank deposits transferable by cheque.

7 Why are coins and banknotes called token money?

Because they have little or no value in themselves. Their only value lies in the fact that they have been declared legal tender.

8 What is legal tender?

A form of payment which by law a creditor must accept in settlement of a debt. In England, Bank of England notes and £1 coins are legal tender up to any amount, but other coins have a limited legal tender.

9 Why do certain coins have limited legal tender?

(a) To protect creditors from being burdened with excessive quantities of coins and (b) to keep coins for their intended use which is to make small payments.

10 What are the legal tender limits?

(a) 20p for bronze coins. (b) £5 for 5p and 10p coins. (c) £10 for 20p and 50p coins.

11 Why are cheques not legal tender?

Legal tender implies that the coin or note is issued by the authority of Parliament. Since cheques may be drawn by anyone, they have no official status. Consequently no one is obliged to accept a cheque and anyone may refuse to do so.

12 What functions does money perform in a modern society?

Money acts as (a) a medium of exchange; (b) a measure of value; (c) a store of value; (d) a standard for postponed payments.

13 What are the qualities of a good monetary medium?

In order to carry out its functions, money must be (a) acceptable; (b) durable; (c) divisible; (d) portable; (e) scarce; (f) homogeneous; (g) difficult to imitate.

14 How do £1 coins possess these qualities?

They are (a) legal tender, so they are acceptable to people in the community; (b) strong and hard wearing; (c) capable of division into small units; (d) easy to carry about; (e) limited in supply; (f) uniform in size and shape; and (g) made of a metal that is not easy to obtain, with a milled edge and a clear and intricate 'head' and 'tail' pattern – so they are difficult to imitate.

15 What is the value of money?

Its purchasing power as represented by the general level of prices. When prices fall, the value of money rises; when prices rise, the value of money falls.

16 What is the General Index of Retail Prices?

An index number published each month by the Department of Employment. It measures the month-to-month changes in the prices of a large and representative selection of goods and services. Thus the Index provides an indication of the way in which retail prices are moving. It can be used to assess changes in the value of money.

17 What is the meaning of 'inflation'?

A situation in which the general level of prices is rising, in other words, the value of money is falling.

Written Exercise: *Why is money essential to a modern economy?*

Go over the topic again until you are sure of all the answers. Then tick it off on the check list at the back of the book.

7 Banks and banking

1 What is a bank?

A business which carries out some or all of the following activities: (a) it accepts deposits for safe-keeping from customers; (b) it enables these customers to make payments through the cheque (and other) systems; (c) it loans funds under certain conditions to those who require them; (d) it assists in making coins and notes available throughout the country.

2 What is the tripartite structure of the English banking system?

(a) *The Bank of England* – the government's bank responsible for the control of the monetary system, including the issue of bank notes and coins. (b) '*Recognised banks*' – in accordance with the Banking Act 1979 only institutions which have been recognised by the Bank of England are entitled to describe themselves as banks. (c) '*Licensed deposit takers*' – institutions which offer a variety of financial services but not a full banking service and therefore may not describe themselves as banks.

3 What are commercial banks?

Public companies such as Barclays, Lloyds, Midland and National Westminster which undertake most kinds of banking business. These banks have branches throughout the country.

4 How do merchant banks differ from commercial banks?

They do not offer the usual commercial banking facilities except on a very limited scale. Based in London, they are specialised banks which assist industry and commerce in particular ways. These include (a) financing of foreign trade; (b) arranging new issues of shares; (c) dealing in foreign exchange; (e) management of investments for pension funds, charities and unit trusts; (f) provision of specialist advice in arranging loans to industry.

5 What is the National Girobank?

A bank set up in 1968 to offer through the Post Office network a more limited range of services than those available from commercial banks. Since then the service has expanded to include provision of: (a) deposit accounts; (b) credit transfers of wages and other moneys; (c) payment orders (which are similar to cheques); (d) standing orders and direct debit transfers; (e) travellers' cheques and foreign currency; (f) a cheque guarantee card which enables cash to be drawn at any post office.

6 Which documents are required to operate a current account?

(a) Paying-in slips; (b) cheques.

7 How do banks earn income?

By investing and lending the surplus money deposited by customers. Additional income is received from charges made for certain services, but the greater part of a bank's earnings arise from charging interest on loans.

8 What are the main forms of advances offered by commercial banks?

(a) Overdrafts. (b) Ordinary loans. (c) Loans for house purchase. (d) Personal loans. (e) Purchase of bills of exchange.

9 Which factors must a bank manager consider before arranging an advance?

(a) Current government policy. (b) The bank's liquidity position. (c) The character of the borrower. (d) The purpose for which the advance is required. (e) The earning power likely to result from the advance. (f) The amount of collateral security available. (g) The proposed duration and rate of repayment.

10 Give examples of collateral security

(a) A life assurance policy that has built up a cash surrender value. (b) Title deeds to property. (c) Government stocks. (d) Shares of public companies. (e) A written undertaking from a guarantor.

11 What is an overdraft?

A method of borrowing from a bank. The borrower is permitted to draw cheques for an agreed amount in excess of the sum deposited in his or her current account.

12 Why is an overdraft a very convenient method of borrowing?

(a) Money is not borrowed until it is actually spent. (b) Payments in to the account automatically reduce the overdraft. (c) There is no fixed schedule of repayments. (d) Interest is charged only on the amount by which the account is actually overdrawn.

13 What is a budget account?

An account designed to assist bank customers with forward budgeting. The customer opens a separate account for use in payment of regular bills (rent, rates, etc.). The account is fed by a monthly transfer from the customer's current account. The amount transferred is sufficient over 12 instalments to cover the whole year's payments. The customer pays bills as they become due. Thus the budget account will be sometimes overdrawn and sometimes in surplus and the cost of regular items of expenditure is spread evenly over the year.

14 What is a night safe?

A facility which enables customers such as shopkeepers who do not end the day's business until after the bank has closed, to deposit money safely.

15 What is a cash dispenser?

A machine which supplies cash at any time to customers who have obtained a cash card from the bank. After insertion of the card the computer checks its validity and invites the customer to key in the code number on the keyboard. A cash pack is then released to the customer, or the customer may be invited to request the release of any sum required up to £100.

16 How does a bank ensure that it can meet customers' demands for cash?

By (a) maintaining a cash reserve and (b) investing a proportion of its deposits in assets which can quickly be turned back into cash. These liquid assets comprise short-term loans 'on call' from the discount houses and gilt-edged brokers, and Treasury, bank and trade bills of exchange. The Bank of England requires all banks to agree with the Bank of England their 'prudential policies' – in other words their prudent behaviour as far as customers' needs are concerned.

Written Exercise: *In what ways are the services provided by the National Girobank (a) similar to, and (b) different from, those offered by the commercial banks?*

Go over the topic again until you are sure of all the answers. Then tick it off on the check list at the back of the book.

8 Settling debts

1 How may debts be settled?

(a) In cash (notes and coins of the realm). (b) By cheque. (c) By electronic transfer, as with the new 'home banking' services. (d) By a range of other financial instruments such as bills of exchange, credit cards, etc. (e) By facilities provided by the Post Office.

2 What is special about cash?

Notes and coins of the realm are designated 'legal tender' and any creditor (a person to whom money is owed) is required by law to accept them in settlement of the debt.

3 Is a cheque legal tender?

No, and therefore a shopkeeper or other creditor can refuse to take a cheque.

4 Who declares coins and notes to be legal tender?

The sovereign power in the country concerned – in the United Kingdom this means the 'Queen in Parliament'.

5 Cheques are dealt with in Topics 9 and 10. List any other payment facilities provided by bankers

(a) Bank giro (credit transfers). (b) Standing orders. (c) Direct debits. (d) Bankers' drafts. (e) Credit cards. (f) Home banking by electronic means.

6 How does 'bank giro' work?

It transfers money within the banking system (there is no need to write a letter to the creditor enclosing a cheque). The bank passes a 'credit transfer' to the creditor's account. The payer's account is debited, or alternatively the money can be paid in cash over the counter. The system is widely used by agents to make payment to mail-order firms.

7 How do 'standing orders' work?

A customer requests the bank to pay regularly (usually every month) a sum to a creditor. Standing orders are used for paying mortages, hire purchase instalments, subscriptions, etc.

8 How do direct debits work?

The opposite way to standing orders. The customer signs an authority to a creditor permitting him/her to ask the bank for money from the customer's account. This method is useful when the sum required is different each time.

9 What is a banker's draft?

A cheque drawn on a bank instead of on a person's account.

10 Why is a draft more acceptable to a creditor than a personal cheque?

A draft is drawn on the bank itself. There is no risk of its being dishonoured because the person obtaining it has already paid the bank the amount of the draft. Drafts may be used to pay a supplier when a new customer has not yet established a record of integrity and proper business conduct.

11 How do cheque cards work?

They are virtually a letter of recommendation by the banker to all traders and banks handling the cards. They say 'this person is reliable to the limit of the value of the card (at the time of writing £50)'. If any difficulty arises the bank honours the payment. A signature is required from the card-holder which must be the same as the signature on the card.

12 How does home banking work?

The householder or office buys a special device from the bank which enables him/her to link up with the bank's computer. By feeding in codes and amounts, the customer's debts are paid instantaneously, the creditor's account being credited and the debtor's account debited immediately.

13 Name the money transfer services available at a Post Office

(a) Postage stamps – for small payments. (b) Postal orders – for amounts up to £10. (c) Overseas money orders. (d) Registered post. (e) Cash on delivery service. (f) National Girobank facilities such as ordinary transfers, girocheques and transcash.

Written Exercise: *Describe three methods of payment which are provided by the commercial banks, other than payment by cheque. In your answer explain the circumstances which make each method convenient for both debtor and creditor.*

Go over the topic again until you are sure of all the answers. Then tick it off on the check list at the back of the book.

9 Cheques and cheque crossings

1 What is a cheque?

It is a bill of exchange drawn on a banker payable on demand. (A bill of exchange is explained later.)

2 Who are the parties to a cheque?

(a) The drawer (the one who writes it out and signs it). (b) The drawee (the one instructed to pay). (c) The payee (the one who is to be paid).

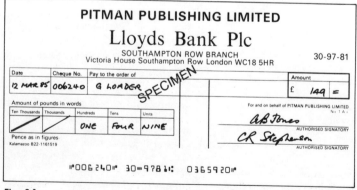

Fig. 9.1

3 Who is the drawer of the cheque in Fig. 9.1?	Pitman Publishing Limited.
4 Who is the drawee?	Lloyds Bank.
5 Who is the payee?	Mr G Loader.
6 What is an order cheque?	A cheque which is payable either to the payee or to anyone else whom the payee orders the bank to pay by endorsement of the cheque.
7 What does endorsement mean?	It means 'writing on the back' (*en dos* in French). For example, Mr Loader might write 'Pay T Smith', and sign the instruction 'G Loader'.
8 What is an open cheque?	An uncrossed cheque which can be cashed at the branch of the bank on which it is drawn, by the person named on the cheque.
9 What is a crossed cheque?	One bearing two parallel lines across the face of the cheque which prevents its being cashed across the counter of a bank (except by the account holder).
10 What kind of crossing is used on the cheque?	A general crossing. This kind of crossing may be just two lines, or two lines with (& Co) or 'not negotiable' or 'account payee only' written between the parallel lines.
11 What is the effect of a general crossing?	The crossing cancels out the order to pay on demand, so that the cheque cannot be cashed immediately across the bank counter. It must always be paid for collection into a bank account but not necessarily into any particular bank account.
12 A cheque is said to be a negotiable instrument. What does this mean?	It mean that – to a person who is behaving in a proper manner and taking the cheque in good faith for value

received – it transfers a good title, even if the person giving the cheque does not have a good title of ownership.

13 How would writing 'not negotiable' protect the drawer of the cheque?

It destroys the concept of negotiability of the cheque. A person taking such a cheque does not get a good title – only the same title as the person giving it – which to a thief means no title at all.

14 Is 'not negotiable' intended to restrict the transferability of a cheque?

No. It acts merely as a warning against accepting such a cheque from someone whose integrity is not known.

15 How does 'Account payee only' act as a safeguard?

Normally the collecting bank will clear the cheque into the account of the named payee only.

16 What is a special crossing?

A crossing with the name of a particular bank written between the parallel lines.

17 What is the effect of a special crossing?

The cheque can be paid in for collection only at the specified bank.

18 Firms which receive large numbers of cheques have to return some of them because they are written incorrectly. List some of the common errors.

(a) Cheque is not signed. (b) Cheque signed by only one person when two signatures are required. (c) Cheque is not dated. (d) The amount in words differs from the amount in figures. (e) The word 'pounds' has been left out in the written amount – for example 'one hundred and eighty 82p' will not do. It must say 'one hundred and eighty *pounds* 82p'. (f) At the start of a year it is quite common for people to write the previous year's date – for example in January 1986 to write '7 January 1985' – which makes the cheque 'stale'.

19 What are the benefits of making payments by cheque?

(a) The risk of robbery when making large cash payments is avoided. (b) Any amount can be paid with a single cheque. (Contrast writing a £10 000 cheque with counting out a thousand

£10 notes.) (c) Another safe feature is that the drawer can direct that a cheque be paid into a particular account at a particular branch of a particular bank (special crossing). (d) The drawer may ask the bank to stop payment if, for example, a cheque is lost in the post. (c) A paid cheque serves as legal evidence of a receipt (in the United Kingdom). (d) Banks keep records of all payments which serve as useful checks for drawers and payees.

Written Exercise: *What are the safeguards that may be used when drawing a cheque? Illustrate your answer by drawing up an imaginary cheque in each of the styles required.*

Go over the topic again until you are sure of all the answers. Then tick it off on the check list at the back of the book.

10 More about cheques

1 What is a bearer cheque and why is it not as safe as an order cheque?

It is a cheque which is worded 'Pay bearer' or 'Pay . . . or bearer' and is payable to anyone who presents the cheque. If lost or stolen and presented to a bank by a person not entitled to present it, the cheque would be cashed.

2 What is a post-dated cheque?

A cheque dated for some time in the future. If presented for payment on or after that date it will be honoured.

3 What is a stale cheque?

A cheque presented for payment more than six months after being drawn. The bank will mark it 'out of date' and decline payment.

4 What is an endorsement?

The signature of the payee with or without instructions written on the back of the cheque. If without any instructions as to whom to pay, it is called an endorsement in blank.

5 What is the effect of endorsement in blank?

The cheque becomes payable to 'bearer' and the bearer may either pay it into an account or pass it on in payment.

6 What is a special endorsement?

The signature of the payee written on the back of the cheque together with the name of the person to whom the cheque is to be paid.

7 What is the effect of a special endorsement?

The bank will pay the cheque as ordered. The new payee must also endorse the cheque if wishing to use it to settle a debt.

8 What is a restrictive endorsement?

The signature of the payee written on the back of the cheque together with an instruction to pay only the person named. The new payee cannot pass on the cheque to anyone else, but must pay it into his/her account.

9 In what circumstances will a bank refuse to pay a cheque?

If the drawer (a) has insufficient funds to meet the cheque or (b) has requested that payment is stopped or (c) becomes bankrupt or dies. In addition, payment will be refused (d) if the signature on the cheque differs from the drawer's specimen signature held by the bank or (e) any alteration on the cheque has not been signed by the drawer or (f) the amount written in words differs from the amount written in figures or (g) the cheque is either stale or post-dated.

Written Exercise: *Draw up three rectangles to represent the back of a cheque. Then write on them in turn as follows: (a) A blank endorsement. (b) An endorsement ordering the bank to pay P Jones. (c) A restrictive endorsement ordering the bank to pay A South.*

Go over the topic again until you are sure of all the answers. Then tick it off on the check list at the back of the book.

11 The Bank of England

1 What is a 'central bank'?

A bank which is at the heart of a country's banking system and plays a major part in administering the government's monetary policy. There is normally only one central bank in each country and in Britain it is the Bank of England. The central bank has a number of special functions.

2 What are the functions of the Bank of England?

(a) To control the issue of notes and coins in England and Wales. (b) To act as banker to the government. (c) To act as banker to the commercial banks. (d) To apply the government's monetary policy. (e) To act as lender of last resort. (f) To exercise a statutory responsibility for oversight of the banking system.

3 How is the Bank concerned with the issue of notes and coins?

The Bank prints notes and authorises the minting of coins by the Royal Mint. New notes and coins are put into circulation in return for old worn out ones which are removed by the commercial banks.

4 Which bank accounts does the Bank administer for the government?

There are two principal accounts: (a) the **Exchequer Account** into which government revenue (such as the proceeds from taxation) is paid and from which payment is made for goods and services received by the government; (b) the **National Loans Fund** through which passes government borrowing and lending. The Bank also keeps the accounts of a number of government departments.

5 What is the National Debt?

The accumulated total of annual borrowings by the government. The management of the National Debt is entrusted to the Bank.

6 How does the Bank arrange loans for the government?

(a) Direct borrowing in the form of ways and means advances is on a relatively small scale. (b) Short-term loans are raised by selling Treasury bills in the money market. (c) Long-term loans are obtained by selling new issues of government stock in the capital market. Registers of stockholders are kept by the Bank, which also pays the interest and arranges transfers and repayments when due. These types of stock are called gilt-edged securities.

7 What other duties does the Bank perform for the government?

(a) It gives advice on general financial matters such as the level of interest rates, the money supply etc. (b) It maintains relations with international monetary authorities (such as the International Monetary Fund) and with the central banks of other countries. (c) It manages the Exchange Equalisation Account – a fund of foreign currencies which can be used to support the pound sterling if it comes under pressure on foreign exchange markets around the world.

8 How does the Bank influence the value of the pound in the foreign exchange markets?

When the value of the pound falls below an acceptable level, the Bank increases demand for pounds by buying them on the market, using for this purpose its stock of foreign currencies. If the value rises above the required level, the Bank sells pounds, and takes in foreign exchange instead, to replenish its reserves.

10 Why is a cheque clearing system necessary?

A cheque can be paid only at the branch on which it is drawn. Therefore, either the payee must take the cheque, if it is not crossed, to that branch for payment in cash, or it must be paid into a bank for collection from the drawer's bank. Most cheques are paid in for collection through the clearing system and a cheque is said to be 'cleared' when it has been paid by the branch on which it was drawn.

11 What is a clearing house?

A place for the settlement of debts, usually by balancing one debt against another and settling the difference. The best-known example is the London Bankers' Clearing House, but other businesses have clearing houses for settlement of the sums due between members, e.g. airline companies, commodity markets, etc.

12 How does the Town Clearing differ from the General Clearing?

At the Bankers' Clearing House, the Town Clearing handles cheques drawn on banks within the City of London area only. All other cheques are cleared through the General Clearing.

13 Does the Bankers' Clearing House deal only with cheques?

No. Bank giro transfers, direct debits, standing orders and other means of payment via the banks also go through the Clearing House.

14 What is the meaning of 'monetary policy'?

Monetary policy is concerned with increasing or reducing the supply of money. Monetary measures are designed to affect the overall level of demand in the economy through influencing the cost of borrowing and the availability of loans. Bank deposits are a major element in the money supply; so monetary controls are intended to regulate bank lending, which influences the money people can spend from their current accounts.

15 What is the aim of contracting the money supply?

The purpose is to deter spending by making finance more expensive and difficult to obtain. Thus demand for goods and services will be reduced and investment will be discouraged. A policy

16 What is an inflationary policy?

that aims to decrease the supply of money in order to reduce the general price level is said to be deflationary.

One that aims to increase the money supply so that spending and investment are encouraged and employment rises.

17 What are the instruments of monetary policy?

(a) Open market operations. (b) Interest rate policy. (c) Special deposits. (d) Directives.

18 What are open-market operations?

The sale or purchase of government securities by the Bank on the Stock Exchange and the money markets generally. For example, if the aim is to contract the money supply, the Bank sells securities. If these are short-term securities (Treasury Bills), they soak up surplus money on the money markets to reduce the money supply. If they are long-term gilt-edged securities, buyers pay by cheques drawn on the commercial banks. The reserve balances held by the commercial banks at the Bank will, therefore, be reduced and in order to maintain liquidity, bank advances must be reduced. This is at present the chief method of influencing the money supply.

19 How can the Bank's controls be used to expand the money supply?

By using the following measures either individually or collectively: (a) purchase of securities on the money markets and the Stock Exchange; (b) reduction of interest rates; (c) release of special deposits (if any have been collected); (d) issue of directives to encourage the adoption of a generous lending policy.

20 How does the Bank act as 'lender of last resort'?

The Bank will always seek to ensure that the banking system can meet its obligations to pay cash to its customers. It is only the discount houses that get into trouble, since a bank in difficulty will simply call the money it has 'at call or short notice' with the discount houses (leaving *them* short of money). In this situation, at 2.30 p.m. every day the discount houses are allowed to ask the Bank for funds to balance their books – and they may be charged a high rate of interest if the Bank wants to 'punish' them for being too generous with their lending policies.

21 How does the Bank exercise its statutory responsibility to oversee the activities of other banks?

The core of this responsibility is to limit as far as possible the risks to a bank's reserves from mismatched or over-concentrated investment or lending. To do this, all banks must agree their prudential policies (their policies for prudent behaviour about reserves) with the Bank of England, and if they get into difficulties must be prepared to explain what happened and to alter their policies immediately.

Written Exercises: *Describe the activities undertaken by the Bank of England in keeping control of the money supply.*

Go over the topic again until you are sure of all the answers. Then tick it off on the check list at the back of the book.

12 Road, Rail and Inland Water Transport

1 What is the relationship between mass production and transport?

The system of mass production relies on an efficient transport system for its existence. Large quantities of goods are produced for consumers situated many miles away from the centre of production.

2 How does transport aid trade?

(a) Supplies of raw materials are moved to where they are needed for manufacture. (b) Finished goods are distributed to wholesalers, retailers and consumers.

3 How do transport costs influence industrial location?

Transport is a major cost of production. The costs of transporting raw materials can be minimised by locating as near to their source as possible or alternatively, the costs of distribution can be reduced by locating as near to the market as possible. The actual course adopted will depend very largely on the nature of the industry, and the nature of the product.

4 What are the options available to a trader who wishes to send goods by road?

(a) The hire of the services of a road haulage firm which might be a local carrier (for short distances) or a general carrier (for longer journeys). (b) The use of the trader's own vehicle.

5 What are the particular benefits of using the trader's own vehicle?

(a) Goods remain under the trader's control until the actual delivery to the buyer. (b) Goods can be sent out at times convenient to both trader and customer. (c) The vehicle can be used to (i) bring back empty containers (if these are used in the business) and (ii) advertise the trader's business.

6 Are there any drawbacks to the use of the trader's own vehicle?

Yes. (a) There is the capital cost of buying the vehicle. (b) The driver's wages and expenses have to be found and (c) unless the vehicle is fully employed, the cost per mile may be higher than the charges of independent carriers.

7 What are the advantages of road transport over rail transport?

(a) *Door-to-door service*: vehicles can travel anywhere where a road exists and a door-to-door service is available. Rail transport has to be completed by a road delivery vehicle. (b) *Flexibility*: road

vehicles can be rerouted to avoid traffic hold-ups, bad weather etc. A train is tied to its permanent way, and a stoppage at any point delays all trains behind – though some rerouting may be possible.
(c) *Speed*: roads are faster than rail for short journeys (less than 200 miles) because no time is lost in changing from one form of transport to another.
(d) *Supervision of the goods*: goods are under the control of the vehicle driver at all times, not waiting relatively unprotected in rail sidings, depots, etc.
(e) *Economy*: road haulage is very competitive and rail transport is a monopoly. As a result, freight rates are usually cheaper by road.

8 In what circumstances does rail transport have advantages over carriage by road?

(a) Over long journeys, railways are faster. (b) A train crew can convey a considerable tonnage in one train load whereas a large numbers of lorries and drivers would be needed to move the same quantity. Thus railways have an advantage for the transport of large quantities of heavy, bulky goods such as coal.

9 What is a freightliner?

A train used to operate a regular rail freight service for the transport of containers.

10 What are containers?

A method of transporting goods by road, rail, sea and air. Goods are packed into a large metal container at the consignor's depot and the container is then transported to its destination as a unit load.

11 What are the particular benefits of the freightliner service?

(a) *Speed*: trains leave on time and travel fast. (b) *Reliability*: scheduled trains enable firms to plan their deliveries with certainty. (c) *Safety*: containers are packed at the consignor's depot and the possibility of pilfering is eliminated. (d) *Large capacity*: the movement of containers by the trainload means that no job is too extensive to tackle. (e) *Reserved space*: train space may be reserved in advance and so eliminate delays at the freightliner terminal.

12 What are inland waterways?

They comprise navigable rivers and canals.

13 Why has the use of inland waterways declined in Britain?

(a) Journey times are slow. (b) In winter the water may freeze and stop journeys. (c) Direct delivery can be made only to places situated on the sides of the waterways. (d) Canals and locks vary in size, so that only a small barge can travel throughout the canal system.

14 Are there any benefits in using inland waterways for transport?

Yes. (a) Low energy costs make for relative cheapness, and water transport is particularly suitable for bulky goods of low value such as coal, sand and bricks. (b) The hinterland becomes accessible by water from the mouths of estuaries, so that ships such as barge carriers can operate.

Written Exercise: *(a) Why do many firms have their own vehicles for delivering goods? (b) For what reasons might a manufacturer decide to use rail transport?*

Go over the topic again until you are sure of all the answers. Then tick it off on the check list at the back of the book.

13 Transport by Sea, Air and Pipeline

1 What are the various types of sea transport?

(a) Tramp ships (b) cargo-passenger ships (c) container ships (d) special-purpose ships such as oil tankers and refrigerated vessels.

2 What are tramp ships?

Vessels which may be chartered (hired) to travel anywhere in the world. They are cargo vessels which have no set routes or times.

3 What is a charter party?

A contract made between a shipowner and a cargo-owner for the use of the vessel to transport cargo.

4 What is the difference between a voyage charter and a time charter?

A voyage charter is the hire of a ship for a particular voyage or number of voyages whereas a time charter is the hire of a ship for a certain period of time regardless of the number of voyages.

5 Name the largest market in the world for the chartering of ships

The Baltic Exchange in London.

6 How does a shipowner sell freight space?

By instructing a shipping broker who meets other brokers who represent prospective charterers of ships. Bargaining between the brokers determines freight rates.

7 How are tramp freight rates determined?

By the demand for and the supply of shipping space.

8 How do cargo-passenger liners differ from tramp ships?

Unlike tramps, liners work to fixed schedules and timetables. They provide shippers of goods with a regular service.

9 How are liners assured of reasonable freight rates?

Liner owners belong to **shipping conferences** which fix rates for carrying cargo. The members meet from time to time to renew and revise existing rates or to compile new ones.

10 How does a shipping conference encourage regular support from shippers?

By establishing 'ties' between shippers and the conference. The tie takes the form of an agreement to ship cargo with conference liners in return for the benefits of regular sailings, preferential rates and sufficient tonnage for normal requirements. A rebate of freight paid is offered on proof that goods have been transported exclusively during the previous trading period by the conference liners.

11 What are the benefits of using containers in sea transport?

(a) Loading times are shorter so that vessels turn round faster and labour handling and port costs are reduced. (b) Containers protect goods from the weather. (c) Containers are sealed with the authority of the Customs which makes pilfering difficult and simplifies Customs procedures at the port of arrival. (d) Freight rates are lower.

12 How can traders charter aircraft?

Through brokers who work at the air freight market at the Baltic Exchange. The procedure at the Exchange is similar to that used for sea freight.

13 What are the advantages of air freight?

(a) Speed of delivery. (b) Aircraft can travel long distances over land and sea without unloading and reloading freight. (c) Reduced packing costs – a smooth passage means that the danger of damage to delicate articles is reduced. (d) Reduced insurance costs – relatively quick journey times mean that shorter periods of cover are required.

14 Are there drawbaks to air transport?

Yes. (a) Bad weather may restrict flights. (b) Airports are situated on the outskirts of towns and goods may have to be

taken a considerable distance by road or rail before and after the flight. (c) Air freight rates are relatively high.
(d) Aircraft have a limited load capacity.

15 Which types of commodities are transported by pipelines?

Liquids such as oil, petrol and water; and gases.

16 What are the attractions of using pipelines for transport?

(a) There is a saving of the fuel costs used in other forms of transport.
(b) Once installed either underground or under the sea, there is less damage to the environment than from other forms of transport. (c) Maintenance costs are relatively low. (d) This is a safe means of transferring inflammable commodities. (e) Transfer continues 24 hours a day.

17 Are there limitations to the use of pipelines?

Yes. (a) The costs of installation.
(b) Installation problems in built up areas. (c) The limited range of commodities which can be transported.
(d) The general restriction in use to a single type of product for each pipeline.

18 Are freight rates the only factor to consider when selecting a method of transport?

No. In addition to the actual rate charged, a trader must consider a number of other factors including:
(a) the nature of the commodity concerned – whether it is bulky, valuable, fragile or perishable; (b) the urgency of delivery; (c) the geographical locations of the consignor and consignee; (d) the quantity of the commodity to be delivered.

Written Exercise: *Goods are carried to London by road, rail, river, canal and air. State with reasons which types of goods are transported by each of these methods.*

Go over the topic again until you are sure of all the answers. Then tick it off on the check list at the back of the book.

14 Communications

1 What is 'communication'?

The word means conveying ideas and information from one person to another. Ideas may be conveyed in either written or spoken form.

2 What forms can spoken communication take?

(a) Personal (face to face) conversation: giving instructions, making requests; engaging in discussions, meetings and conferences. (b) Telephone conversation using either the British Telecom network or an internal intercom system. (c) Mass media systems such as public address systems, radio and television.

3 What forms can written communication take?

(a) Personal communications within an organisation by memoranda, bulletins, notices, house journals, etc. (b) Personal external communications by letters, press releases, reports, cables, telexes, facsimile copying, etc. (c) Mass media communications by press advertisements, posters, public notices, etc.

4 How do modern means of communication assist commerce?

(a) Information concerning the state of the market – whether there is an abundance or shortage of a commodity – enables those engaged in commerce to move goods efficiently to where they are required. (b) Telephone and telex services enable traders to make immediate contact even though they are situated thousands of miles apart.
(c) Postal systems provide a means for the transfer of documents used in business transactions.

5 What does 'post office preferred' (POP) mean?

The phrase refers to an internationally agreed range of standardised shapes and sizes for letter envelopes and cards. The purpose is to facilitate machine sorting of mail.

6 When is a postcard used rather than a letter?

A postcard is used for messages (a) that are short, such as orders for goods or acknowledgement of receipt and (b) are not of a private nature.

7 What is a postcode and what is its purpose?

A group of letters or figures which represents an address in abbreviated form as an aid to the automatic sorting of mail. The first part represents the postal delivery district of the town and the second the street, part of street or even building where the letter has to be delivered.

8 How can urgently required letters be sent quickly?

By use of (a) the express and special delivery services available through the Post Office or (b) private postal services. The latter provide (i) conveyance around London and other large cities by motorcycle or van; (ii) guaranteed overnight deliveries throughout Britain; (iii) 24-hour international deliveries.

9 What is the business-reply service?

A service available under licence from the Post Office to firms wishing to encourage replies from clients by not putting them to the expense of paying postage. The addressee pays the postage on all the replies received.

10 What is telex?

A public teleprinter service operated by British Telecom. The operation of a teleprinter permits immediate reproduction of information on both transmitting and receiving machines.

11 What are the advantages of telex?

(a) Reports can be communicated quickly over long distances. (b) The printing of simultaneous copies at both the transmitting and the receiving end reduces any risk of mistakes and misunderstandings. (c) Messages can be received even when a business office is closed.

Written Exercise: *List the methods of communication available for business purposes through the Post Office and British Telecom. Which method would be appropriate for (a) urgent messages (b) safe delivery of documents (c) immediate access to an international destination for a written message?*

Go over the topic again until you are sure of all the answers. Then tick it off on the check list at the back of the book.

15 Sole Traders, Partnerships and Cooperatives

1 What is a sole trader?

A form of business organisation in which the one owner (a) is responsible for raising the capital; (b) manages the business; (c) takes all the profit or bears responsibility if the business suffers a loss. A sole trader pays income tax and national insurance contributions as a self-employed person.

2 Why is the sole trader the most widely used form of business organisation?

(a) Such a business is easy to establish with few formalities. (b) There is no separation of ownership and control. (c) There is personal contact with both customers and employees. (d) There are personal and material rewards in being 'ones own boss'.

3 Are there any problems associated with this form of business?

Yes. (a) Unlimited liability. (b) A lack of continuity of business on the owner's death. (c) Scarcity of capital may limit business development. (d) The owner has to undertake all aspects of the work and a lack of expertise in some areas may lower the operating efficiency of the business.

4 What is 'unlimited liability'?

The personal responsibility of a business owner for all business debts to the full extent of his or her personal wealth.

5 What is a partnership?

A group of people who carry on business with the purpose of making a profit. There are two types of partnership; (a) limited partnerships, (b) ordinary partnerships.

6 How do limited partnerships differ from ordinary partnerships?

In an ordinary partnership, all partners share the profits and each is equally responsible for *all* partnership debts – not merely his or her investment. Under the Limited Partnership Act 1907, a limited partner's liability for the debts of the firm is restricted to the amount of capital personally invested. However, limited partners lose the right to manage the business, and in a limited partnership there must be at least one ordinary partner whose liability is unlimited. Limited partnerships are quite rare.

7 How many people may form a partnership?

Generally, the number may vary from a minimum of two to a maximum of twenty. There is no limit to the number of members of (a) *ordinary partnerships* of solicitors, accountants, stockbrokers and stockjobbers, and (b) *limited partnerships* of surveyors, auctioneers, valuers and estate agents.

8 How is a partnership formed?

By verbal or written agreement. The latter is more usual and certainly desirable. The written terms and conditions of the partnership may take the form of a deed of agreement. This is a formal agreement drawn up by a solicitor and includes such items as the names of the partners, the amount of capital contributed by each, and the arrangements for sharing of profits or losses.

9 How are the rights and duties of partners determined if there is no agreement beforehand?

They are determined by the provisions of the Partnership Act 1890 which states, for example, that if there is no agreement, profits and losses must be divided equally. The Act acts residually; that is, its rules apply to anything the partners overlooked in their agreement.

10 In what ways are sole traders and partnerships similar?

Both the sole trader and the partners (a) provide the capital; (b) operate the business; (c) carry the risks; (d) are able to take decisions quickly because of personal contact with customers and employees; (f) cease to exist with the death of the trader or one of the partners; (g) do not have to file accounts with any authority, such as the Registrar of Companies; (h) bear unlimited liability – unless the partnership is registered as a limited partnership, when the general partner(s) only have unlimited liability.

11 Why might a sole trader wish to form a partnership?

There are certain benefits to be gained: (a) an increase in the capital available; (b) an imporvement in management through the introduction of partners with specialist skills; (c) business efficiency may be improved (i) through the admission of partners with new ideas and thinking, and (ii) by the sharing of responsibilities.

12 Are there any particular drawbacks of partnerships not already mentioned in Question 10?

Yes. (a) Any partner may bind the firm in trading contracts and in this way commit the other partners. Thus a partner with faulty business judgement or low integrity could ruin the business by unwise actions. (b) The consent of all partners is required for the admission of a new partner, and individual obstinacy could very well hinder development of the partnership by refusing the admission of 'new blood'. (c) Except for certain professions the number of partners is limited to twenty. The amount of capital subscribed by even twenty partners may not allow the business to expand to its fullest extent.

13 For which kinds of business is a partnership particularly suitable?

(a) Partnerships exist where professional skill is of greater importance than capital. People who sell services require relatively little capital compared to those who produce goods. (b) Some professional people, e.g. accountants and solicitors, are obliged to work in partnerships because rules made by their governing bodies do not allow members to form limited companies.

14 What are the main sources of finance for sole traders and partnerships?

(a) Personal savings. (b) Loans from friends, a bank or a building society. (c) Factoring. (d) Hire purchase. (e) Leasing. (f) Trade credit. (g) Ploughing back a portion of profits to increase the capital available.

15 What is factoring?

Factoring is the sale of trade debts to a specialist firm known as a factor. Factoring provides the seller of the debts with rapid payment (and hence, finance) and an insurance against bad debts. A variation of this practice, known as invoice discounting, is borrowing against the security of book debts.

16 How does leasing differ from hire purchase?

Whereas under *hire purchase*, the user of the item concerned eventually becomes the owner, under leasing this is not generally the case. A lease is a contract giving the use of equipment for a certain period of time. The lessee pays

17 What are cooperatives?

rent to the owner (or lessor) and ownership remains with the latter.

There are two main types: (a) worker cooperatives and (b) consumer cooperatives. The latter are best known and cooperative retail societies are found throughout the United Kingdom.

18 What is a workers' cooperative?

(a) A business owned and controlled by the members who are mainly or entirely employees. (b) The workers provide the capital, take all the management decisions and share out the profits on some agreed basis. (c) Most cooperatives register under the Friendly Societies Acts as corporate bodies with limited liability. (d) They are involved in a wide range of activities such as clothing manufacture and building services. (e) Since the mid-1970s there has been a considerable revival of interest in this form of business and in 1978 the government established a special agency to assist worker cooperatives with advice.

19 What are the benefits of worker cooperatives?

(a) Enhanced job satisfaction.
(b) Minimal conflict, because workers and owners are one and the same.
(c) Increased personal motivation results in goods or services of high quality.
(d) Members obtain an awareness of business realities such as competition.

20 How do cooperative businesses differ from other kinds of business?

Cooperatives operate on these principles: (a) membership is open to all employees; (b) members have equal voting rights – 'one member one vote' – irrespective of their capital contribution; (c) the return on any investment in the cooperative is limited to a reasonable rate; (d) profits are distributed according to work put in, not according to money invested.

Written Exercise: *How do worker cooperatives compare with partnerships with regard to (i) ownership and control of the business, (ii) methods of obtaining capital, (iii) disposal of profits?*

Go over the topic again until you are sure of all the answers. Then tick it off on the check list at the back of the book.

16 Limited liability companies

1 What is a limited company?

A group of people who have joined together in order to carry out some kind of business enterprise, the management of the firm being in the hands of a director or board of directors. The word 'limited' means that each member's liability is limited to the amount of his or her shareholding.

2 How is a company formed?

(a) The promoters of the company submit the following documents (among others) to the Registrar of Companies: (i) a Memorandum of Association; (ii) Articles of Association. (b) If the Registrar is satisfied, a **certificate of incorporation** is issued which gives the company a legal existence. A private company can now start business but a public company still has to obtain its capital from the public before it can commence business. (c) When the Registrar is satisfied that the company's share capital meets the necessary legal requirements, a **trading certificate** is issued. This entitles the public company to commence business.

3 What is a Memorandum of Association?

A document which expresses the intention of the founder members to combine together to form a company and the objects of the company thus set up. It also states (a) the company's name and address; (b) its proposed authorised capital; (c) that the liability of the members is limited; (d) the names and addresses of the first director(s) and the secretary.

4 What are Articles of Association?

These are a set of rules to govern the internal workings of a company. They regulate: (a) the issue and transfer of shares; (b) the holding of meetings of shareholders; (c) the powers and duties of directors; (d) many other matters.

5 What are the main differences between private and public companies?

(a) A public company must have a minimum issued share capital of £50 000; for a private company there is no specified minimum. (b) A public company must have the abbreviation 'PLC' after its name; a private company end with the words 'company limited'. (c) A public company may advertise its shares to the general public; a private company cannot do this. (d) A public company must have a trading certificate from the Registrar before it can commence trading; this is not required for a private company.

6 What is share capital?

Money subscribed to a company by its shareholders. It may consist of (a) ordinary, (b) preference, and (c) deferred shares. There are various types of shares within each of these broad categories. A shareholder is a part owner of the company and is entitled to receive a share of the company's profits in the form of a dividend, if the directors recommend a distribution.

7 What is authorised capital?

(a) The amount of capital stated in the company's Memorandum of Association as the maximum amount authorised to be issued. (b) It is known also as nominal or registered capital. (c) It may be increased by a simple procedure and notification to the Registrar of Companies.

8 What is issued capital?

The capital represented by the number of shares actually issued by a company. It may be the same or less than the authorised capital.

9 What is paid-up capital?

When shares are issued, the company does not always require the full amount to be paid immediately. The proportion of issued capital that is actually paid for is the paid-up capital of the company.

10 What are ordinary shares?

Shares which are ordinarily issued on commencement of a company. They participate equally in the profits of the company and in any residual value if the company is dissolved. Hence they are called **'equities'**. Other shares such as **preference shares**, take precedence over ordinary shares. Holders of ordinary shares are paid a dividend only after the claims of preference shareholders have been met. In a poor trading year, the dividend may be low or non-existent. Thus ordinary shareholders run greater risks than preference shareholders and in consequence usually have superior voting rights.

11 What are preference shares?

These shares have first claim on any profits and normally receive a fixed rate of dividend. In the event of the winding up of the company, preference shareholders usually rank before ordinary shareholders for return of capital. As preference shareholders run less risk, they have less favourable voting rights than other shareholders.

Most issues of preference shares are **cumulative**, i.e. if in any year there are insufficient profits to pay the preference dividend, the amount owing is carried forward until the company is able to pay. **Participating preference shares** receive not only a fixed dividend if the directors recommend a dividend, but also entitle their holders to a further share of profits once they reach a certain level.

12 What are deferred shares?

This class of share (known also as founders' or management shares) is comparatively rare. No dividend is paid until all other types of shares have been paid a certain amount first. The shares are issued to the founders of a business often when it becomes a public company because the valuable voting rights attaching to them enable the founders to retain control. Taking deferred shares also proves the founders' confidence in the future of the firm.

13 What are the ways in which a company can issue shares?

(a) By a **public issue** – the public are invited through a **prospectus** to apply for any number of shares at a fixed price per share. The price may be at **par** (the face value of the share) or at a **premium** (more than the face value. Alternatively the offer may be by **tender**. Here the applicant is invited to write in the price he/she is prepared to pay, e.g. £1.20 for a £1 share. When all bids have been received, the shares are issued at a price that just disposes of the shares. Shares may not be issued at a discount (less than their face value). (b) Through an **offer for sale** – the issue is bought by a merchant bank or stockbroker and then all or part is offered to the public at a slightly higher price. (c) By means of a **placing** – a stockbroker may buy a block of shares from a company in order to resell to clients. (d) By **'rights'** issues – new shares are offered to existing shareholders at a price lower than the current market price. The shareholder may either buy the shares or sell the 'rights' on the stock exchange to someone else who is interested – the sale price reflecting the difference between the issue price and the market price.

14 What are the stages in a public issue of shares?

(a) The prospectus is published with an application form. (b) On application, investors are required to send the application money, which varies from the full amount to a small fraction, say 25 per cent. (c) An allotment meeting is held and the shares are allotted. (d) Allotment letters are posted to the successful applicants, who must then send in a further portion (if necessary) called the allotment money. Letters of regret are sent to unsuccessful applicants. (e) Any balance owing is payable by a number of **calls**. Payment for shares may, therefore, be spread over a period of months.

15 Why might an issue of shares be underwritten?

In return for a commission, a financial institution underwrites or agrees to take a stated proportion of the issue not subscribed by the public. Thus the promoters of the company protect themselves against failure to obtain the capital required.

16 What are debentures?

They are long-term loans to a company and are normally secured against the firm's property (i.e. **mortgage debentures**). Thus in the event of failure to pay the interest the debenture holders can realise the assets and are almost

51

certainly assured of a return of the loan. A fixed rate of interest is paid each year and if the company fails to pay, the debenture holders can force the company into liquidation. Like shares, debentures may be bought and sold on a stock exchange.

17 How do debentures differ from shares?

(a) Debentures holders are not members of the company and do not have voting rights. (b) They receive a fixed rate of interest rather than dividends. (c) The interest is payable whether the company makes profits or not and before any dividend is paid on shares. (d) The debenture holders are secured creditors of the company.

18 What sources of long-term finance (other than shares) are available to a company?

(a) Debentures. (b) Borrowings from banks, merchant banks and finance corporations such as Investors in Industry. (c) Official aid if a firm is located in an area of high unemployment.

19 What are the advantages of limited companies?

(a) Limited liability for shareholders. (b) Unlike sole traders and partnerships, a company has an independent legal existence unaffected by changes of individual shareholders. (c) Larger amounts of capital can be raised than is possible with other forms of business organisation. (d) The division of capital into different kinds of shares, each of which carries a different degree of risk, means that an appeal is made to different groups of investors. (e) **Public companies** have additional benefits: (i) an appeal may be made to the public for funds; (ii) shareholders may easily dispose of or add to their stock of shares through trading on stock exchanges.

20 Are there drawbacks to the company form of organisation?

Yes. (a) Ownership and control become separated. Whereas assets are owned by the shareholders, it is the directors who control policy. (b) The distribution of dividends is subject to the recommendation of the directors who may control more than 51 per cent of the voting shares and therefore cannot be controlled by minority shareholders.

21 Are there drawbacks to public companies?

Yes. (a) The large size of some companies may create problems of management. (b) The personal element which is characteristic of small business organisations may be lacking. (c) The major concern of most shareholders is the amount of dividend. They may show little interest in other factors such as employees' working conditions. (d) The formalities of setting up the company are relatively involved and expensive.

22 What is a multinational company?

A company which owns assets, manufactures and trades in more than one country. Multinational companies can be very rich and powerful.

Written Exercise: *(a) Why is a limited company the most popular form of business organisation for traders and manufacturers? (b)How do public companies differ from consumer cooperatives in (i) ownership and (ii) control?*

Go over the topic again until you are sure of all the answers. Then tick it off on the check list at the back of the book.

17 Public enterprise

1 What is the difference between public and private enterprise?

(a) *Public enterprise* is the production of goods and services by undertakings owned by the state or by local authorities. (b) *Private enterprise* is production by privately owned firms – sole traders, partnerships, limited companies and cooperatives.

2 What are the main forms of public enterprise?

(a) Public corporations. (b) Municipal undertakings.

3 What is a public corporation?

A form of business organisation set up by an Act of Parliament. Each corporation has (a) an independent legal structure, (b) a chairman and members appointed by a government minister, (c) answerability to Parliament through the minister and the submission of accounts to the Public Accounts Committee. Examples of public corporations include British Rail, the Post Office, the Port of London Authority and the Bank of England.

4 What do public corporations do?

They carry out some important function which for one reason or another is not appropriate to the private enterprise sector, in the general way Parliament has deemed to be desirable. They may (a) sell goods or services *directly* to the public, e.g. (i) the nationalised industries which supply coal, electricity etc., (ii) the services of the Post Office; (b) provide services without making a *direct* charge, e.g. BBC, IBA; (c) provide services to specialist sectors of industry and commerce, i.e. Bank of England, various port authorities, etc.

5 What is nationalisation?

The taking over by the State of established industries which were being run as private concerns. In Britain major sections of the fuel, power, transport and steel industries became nationalised industries during the period 1945–51.

6 What is privatisation?

The reverse of nationalisation. It is the selling off, by the State, of nationalised industries for operation as private enterprises (e.g. in 1984 British Telecom was launched as a private company).

7 How are public corporations made accountable to Parliament?

Control is exercised as follows: (a) Each corporation is required to prepare an annual report and submit it to the appropriate minister who may be questioned on it in Parliament. (b) Each corporation's annual accounts are examined by the Public Accounts Committee of the House of Commons. (c) Select Committees (i.e. special parliamentary committees) are empowered to conduct investigations into the workings of the corporations.

8 How do public corporations obtain capital?

The original assets were acquired when the industry was taken over at nationalisation. The purchase was made by the issue of gilt-edged stock, e.g. British Transport Stock. The interest on this stock has to be paid for out of the profits of the industry – a heavy burden. In some cases the government has had to find the money from taxation. Other capital is acquired from a number of sources: (a) from 'profits', (b) by issuing stock to the general public, (c) by grants and loans from the government, (d) by loans (guaranteed by the government) from countries abroad, (e) by short-term borrowing from the banks.

9 How are 'profits' used?

'Profit' cannot be distributed as dividends because there are no shareholders. Instead it is used (a) to pay interest on the stock issued to purchase the business originally or to raise capital since, (b) for expansion, (c) to repay loans to reduce the corporation's debts. Any surplus goes to the government's Exchequer Account.

10 How are losses financed?

Losses are financed by the taxpayers via government grants.

11 What is the role of consumers' consultative councils?

These councils have been established for public corporations to represent consumers' interests. Members are appointed by a government minister. The council's work is (a) to deal with complaints and suggestions from consumers; (b) to advise the minister of consumers' views. Thus, for example, the Post Office Users National Council makes representations to the Post Office on behalf of the customers.

12 What is a municipal undertaking?

A trading enterprise operated by a local authority. Examples include the Birmingham Municipal Bank, swimming baths, theatres, car-parks and markets.

13 How is a municipal undertaking controlled?

Control is exercised through a council committee which delegates authority for the day-to-day running to local government officers. The latter are answerable to the committee for all matters affecting the undertaking.

14 How are profits used and losses financed?

(a) **Profits** made by municipal undertakings may be used to relieve the rates. (Rates are a source of local authority income levied at so much in the pound on the rateable value of property within its area). (b) **Losses** are paid for out of the rates.

15 What are the main arguments used in favour of public enterprise?

(a) Where an industry is a 'natural' monopoly, e.g. the railways (it would be uneconomic to build 3 or 4 lines from A to B) exploitation may occur and social ownership is desirable. (b) Where an industry exploits the gifts of nature which all are entitled to share (i.e. coal), social ownership is desirable. (c) The working of an industry can be planned as a whole, thus avoiding a waste of resources, e.g. duplication of railway lines, gas mains, etc. (d) Account can be taken of objectives other than profit, e.g. a local authority may subsidise swimming facilities because an 'economic' charge could deprive poorer people of the use of the facility. (e) Private ownership of basic industries (i.e. industries on which many other industries depend) might result in exploitation through excessively high prices. (f) Successful municipal trading enterprises may lead to a reduction in the rates. Low rates in a district may attract new industries and so increase prosperity.

16 What are the main criticisms of public undertakings?

(a) The immense size of nationalised industries creates problems of management and control. (b) Salaried managers may show less drive and initiative than those whose own capital is at risk. (c) Lack of competition may lead to inefficiency and higher prices than would be the case under private enterprise. (d) Taxpayers who subsidise nationalised industries do not have the same opportunities for criticism as do shareholders in a limited company.

17 What is a mixed enterprise?

An undertaking in which public authorities and private interests combine to provide capital. For example the government holds shares in some public companies, e.g. British Petroleum PLC.

Written Exercise: *Give an example of (a) a public limited company, (b) a public corporation. Describe how they differ in respect of (i) provision of capital, (ii) ownership, (iii), control, (iv) distribution of profit.*

Go over the topic again until you are sure of all the answers. Then tick it off on the check list at the back of the book.

18 Public sector expenditure and income

1 What are the main items of government expenditure?

(a) *Social services* such as education, health and welfare and social security. (b) *Defence*. (c) *Environmental services*, i.e. spending on roads, law and order, housing and the arts. (d) *National Debt* interest.

2 How does the Government finance its expenditure?

By (a) proceeds from taxation (b) borrowing in the form of (i) Government stocks (ii) Treasury bills (iii) National Savings.

3 What are direct taxes?

(a) Those levied on the income or wealth of persons and firms. (b) They are paid directly by those assessed to the Board of Inland Revenue. (c) The main direct taxes are Income Tax, Corporation Tax, Capital Gains Tax and Capital Transfer Tax.

4 What are indirect taxes?

(a) Those levied on spending on goods and services. (b) They are paid indirectly by consumers in the form of higher prices. (c) The main indirect taxes are customs and excise duties; Value Added Tax; licences for motor vehicles, television and dogs; betting duties on gambling activities. (d) Indirect taxes are collected by the Board of Customs and Excise.

5 What is the National Budget?

(a) An estimate of Government expenditure and revenue for the financial year which runs from 6th April to the following 5th April. (b) The Budget statement is presented to Parliament by the Chancellor of the Exchequer. (c) The Chancellor reports also on the actual expenditure and revenue for the year which has just ended as compared with the previous Budget estimates. (d) Budget Day is the normal occasion when taxation changes are announced. (e) Sometimes interim budgets are introduced at other times during the year.

6 How does the Government forecast expenditure during the next financial year?

(a) The broad outlines are budgeted ahead for the next five years in a rolling budget which reflects Government policies, international commitments on defence, etc. These are published once a year in a White Paper on Public Expenditure. (b) Government departments calculate how much they will need for their work in the year ahead and these figures are called the *estimates*. (c) Estimates have to be approved by the Treasury (the Government department which ensures that the proposed spending is in line with agreed policy). (d) After gaining Treasury approval, the estimates go before Parliament for approval.

7 How does the National Budget differ from a personal budget?

Governments work the opposite way from individuals. Whereas a person plans spending on the basis of a known net income, the Government decides first on expenditure and then announces in the Budget ways in which the expenditure will be financed.

8 What was the original purpose of the Budget?

To enable the Government to raise sufficient revenue to cover expenditure in the same financial year.

9 What are the main purposes of modern budgets?

With the development of Government control of the economy, the Budget has become an important instrument of economic policy. Two main purposes are to assist in (a) the regulation of the economy and (b) the redistribution of income among the various sections of the community.

10 What are the main items of local government expenditure?

The main services provided by local authorities are (a) education (b) police, fire and ambulance (c) health (e) social services (f) parks and libraries (g) highways and lighting (h) housing.

11 How does local government finance its expenditure?

By (a) Government grants (b) miscellaneous income from services, e.g. council house rents (c) rates.

12 What are rates?

(a) Local taxes levied by local authorities on occupiers of property. (b) Every type of property – houses, trade and industrial premises – within the area is given a rateable value and rates are paid in proportion to the rateable value.

Written Exercise: *(a) Describe the sources of income of (i) the central government (ii) local government. (b) Draw up a list of all taxes – direct and indirect – paid by your family.*

Go over the topic again until you are sure of all the answers. Then tick it off on the check list at the back of the book.

Special Note: Revise and Test Commerce 2

As yet your revision of the Commerce syllabus is incomplete, as it proved impossible to revise all the topics in a single booklet. If you have found this book helpful we hope you will continue your revision using Commerce 2. The subjects covered are:

Stock exchanges; insurance; trade; exporting; importing; international payments; credit trading; advertising; consumer protection; earnings; rates and taxes; business documentation.